LEARNING. services

01726 226787
learning.centre5@
st-austell.ac.uk

Cornwall College St Austell
Learning Centre – Level 5

This resource is to be returned on or before the last date stamped below. To renew items please contact the Centre

Three Week Loan

D1330967

CARTOONING FUNDAMENTALS

CARTOONING FUNDAMENTALS

AL ROSS

STRAVON EDUCATIONAL PRESS
New York, N.Y.

Library of Congress Cataloging in Publication Data

Roth, Abraham, 1911-
   Cartooning fundamentals.

   Includes index.
   1. Cartooning.   I. Title.
NC1320.R67   741.5   77-1201
ISBN 0-87396-080-7

Printed in the United States of America

For Sylvia, to whom I owe all my OK's.

CONTENTS

INTRODUCTION

THE BASIC ELEMENT BEHIND GOOD STYLE in cartooning is proper training. Another prerequisite is complete dedication to the art form. In the pages that follow you will be exhorted to be constantly drawing—drawing from the model, sketching and copying the masters, and doodling, a form of subconscious art that helps tap the imagination. These activities will help you achieve your desired goal: mastery of sound cartooning fundamentals.

During a career of cartooning spanning over thirty years, my own style progressed through five or six stages. However, you will not become a cartoonist by copying my style or the style of another. The purpose of this book is to create in you a stimulus, a desire, and an enthusiasm to cartoon as a form of artistic self-expression.

The training for any specialization in art should be fine art. Just as laboratory work is the foundation for all applied science, so fine art is the source of all applied art. The beginning of all art is found in the history of the creative activity of mankind, which developed over thousands of years. Knowledge of this history and of its content should constitute an essential segment of the basic training for all cartoonists.

The illustrations from the masters, which are part of this book, are designed to demonstrate the masters' drawing techniques in relation to cartooning, and to lead you to museums where you can see, enjoy, and learn from the original art of many more of the modern and old masters. Your cartooning can only benefit from such activity.

Finally, I cannot stress too strongly the value of carrying a sketchbook at all times. In it you can record notes, ideas and, above all, a continuous record of your development as a cartoonist.

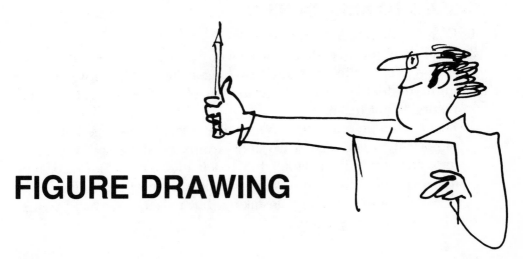

FIGURE DRAWING

DRAWING FROM THE MODEL is important in helping to form a style of cartooning, of illustration, or, for that matter, of fine art. Join a sketch class where models are utilized to pose once, twice, or several times each week. If none is available, or you cannot afford the fee, you can get a friend or members of your family to pose.

It is a good idea to begin the session by limbering up with exercises like these:

THINGS TO KEEP IN MIND

1. Observe the model carefully.
2. Make only positive statements, even if they seem less than accurate. Go over the lines again and again in an affirmative manner until you feel you have the character of the pose. Hesitant statements do not teach.
3. Don't attempt immediately to make a good drawing; it is more important to get a good workout exercise. Make accurate drawings only once in a while; too much effort to achieve accurate drawing will tighten you up, make you sort of muscle-bound. The drawings should not be painstaking, but rather honest and free.

A rapid sketch, establishing the true attitude of the pose immediately, at the same time giving solidity to the chest, torso, and legs.

Avoid academic drawing. The quick sketch will teach you more in the long run. Look first for important elements and disregard detail and minor aspects. It is better to block in the bulk and action of a torso than to differentiate the five fingers of a hand. The proper tilt and structure of the head becomes more important than working out the convolutions of an ear. The eye is easily seduced by detail, but it must be trained to look for the big, simple forms that underlie the details.

Draw the entire figure as quickly as possible, stressing the important lines of action without stopping to put in the details. Do not begin the details before the main direction of your design is satisfied. If you feel like it, do several quick drawings such as the small sketches on this and the following pages.

Here is a quick sketch of
the model bending down.
It was made by using a dry
brush with a minimum of
line.

Concentrate on the main line of the pose—that is, the longest line of the figure—then add the opposing lines. These lines will become the structure to the drawing. Do several rapid drawings of the same pose. You will soon find that the more drawings you do, the more you will be able to create a sense of solidity to the figure.

Have the model take numerous poses. Remember, disregard detail. Just emphasize the main flow of the action of the pose.

Gesture drawings are quick impressions, with the emphasis on the essentials. Each of these took three minutes.

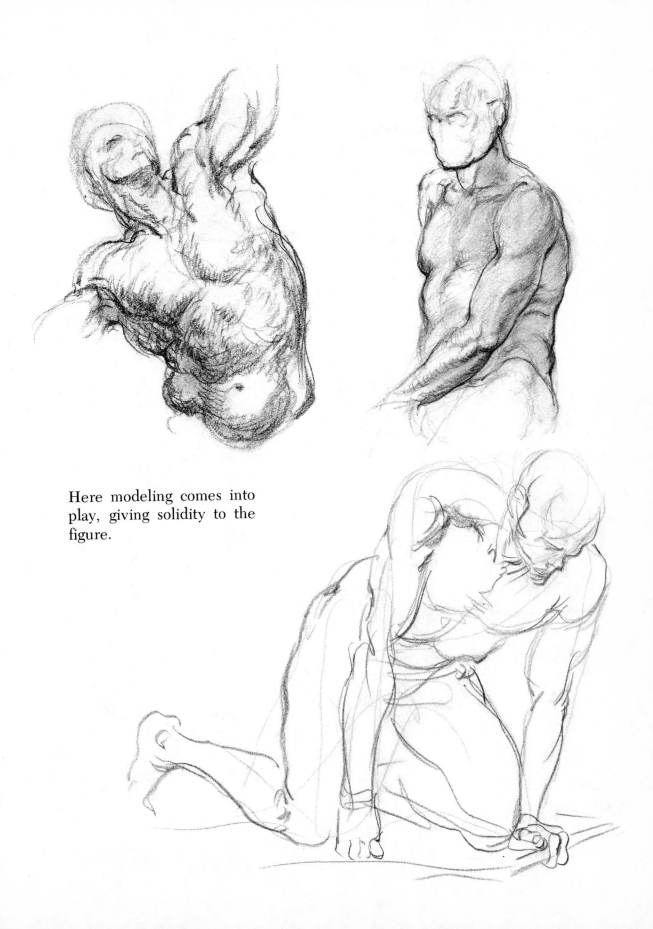

Here modeling comes into play, giving solidity to the figure.

CONTOUR DRAWING

Contour drawing is all linear. The line outlines the form, and is hardly ever shaded. This is probably the fastest way of working.

It should be developed rapidly and naturally. Use a pen or pencil. Don't erase or redo. Use the tool at hand spontaneously.

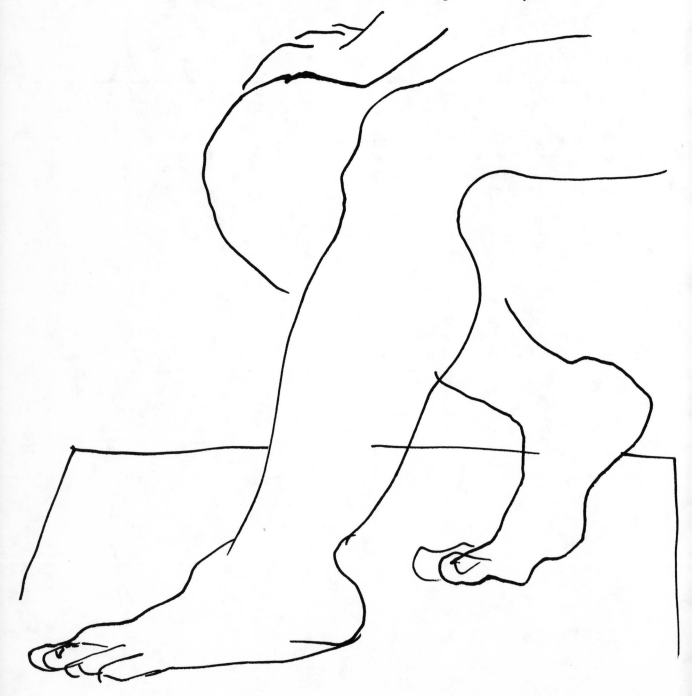

Spontaneous exaggeration imparts a monolithic feeling to the figure.

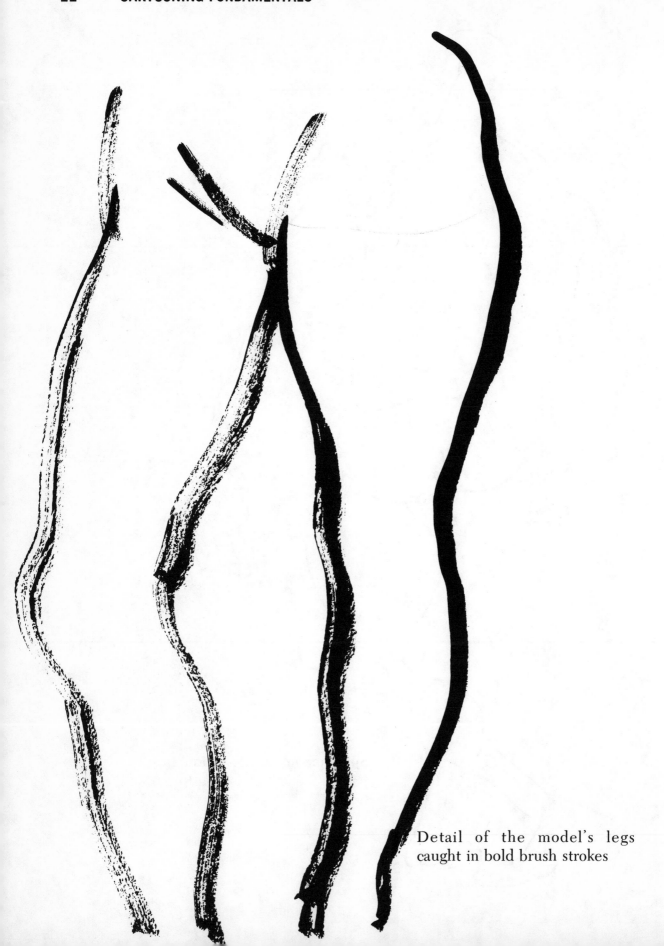

Detail of the model's legs
caught in bold brush strokes

Some heads in various media

Clothing on the model. The form is suggested underneath the clothing; which is, after all, just drapery over the nude body. Here the model has been exaggerated to the point of caricature.

Note how the clothing hugs the figure, revealing the form.

MODEL IN ACTION

In drawing cartoons, you will be utilizing the figure in a great many different actions. Working from the model in poses of this kind is great training for the forming of a cartoon style.

Action includes attitude, emotion, gesture, and expression. If you can feel the action in your own muscles and bones, and then can combine that feeling with your knowledge of the figure, you are apt to get good results in drawing the model in action.

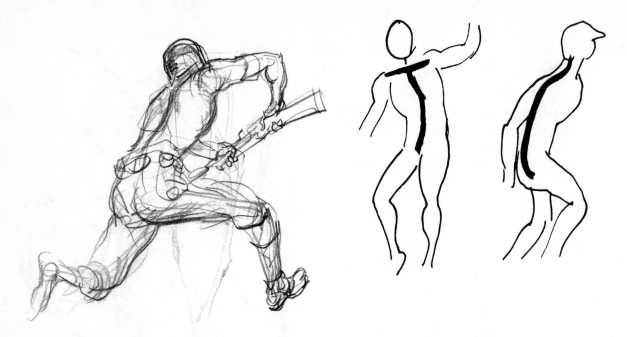

Try to visualize the action of the spine. Even just shifting a foot will cause a slight readjustment of the spine. In the section on anatomy you will observe that the spine serves as a connecting rod between the pelvis, the upper torso, and the head. Once you understand the functions of the spine, the motions of the body become much clearer.

Brush accents help give dynamic
movement to the body.

ANATOMY

It is important to gain an insight into the structure of the human figure. This leads to an understanding of the figure when drawing from the model and in the process of sketching, and eventually to a larger range of fluidity in drawing your cartoon characters and creating a personal cartoon style. A book dealing exclusively with anatomy should be always within reach.

This chapter will deal with a few important anatomical problems in doing illustrations.

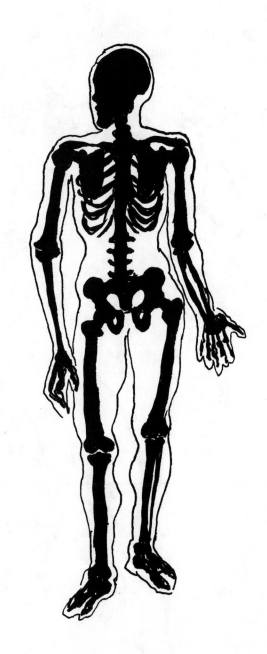

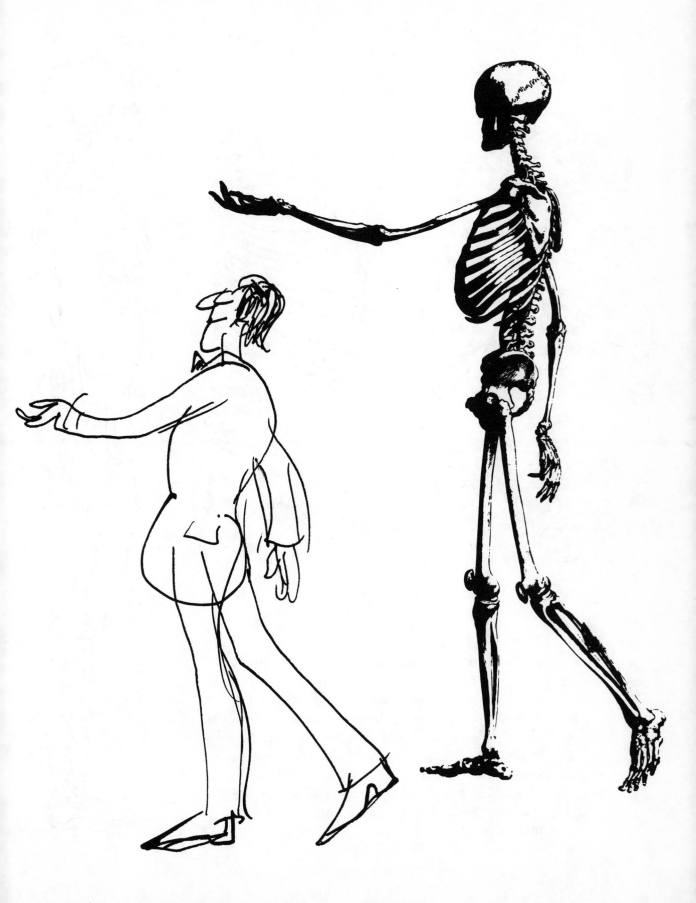

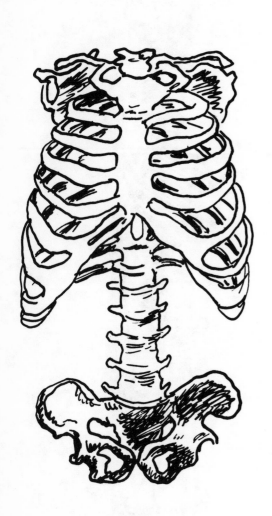

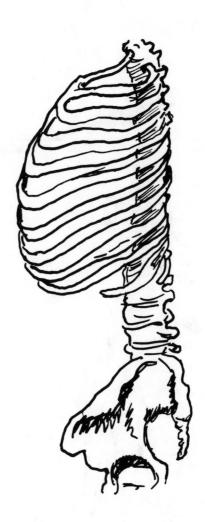

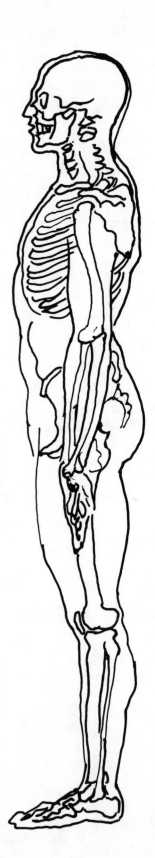

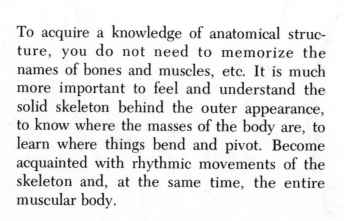

To acquire a knowledge of anatomical structure, you do not need to memorize the names of bones and muscles, etc. It is much more important to feel and understand the solid skeleton behind the outer appearance, to know where the masses of the body are, to learn where things bend and pivot. Become acquainted with rhythmic movements of the skeleton and, at the same time, the entire muscular body.

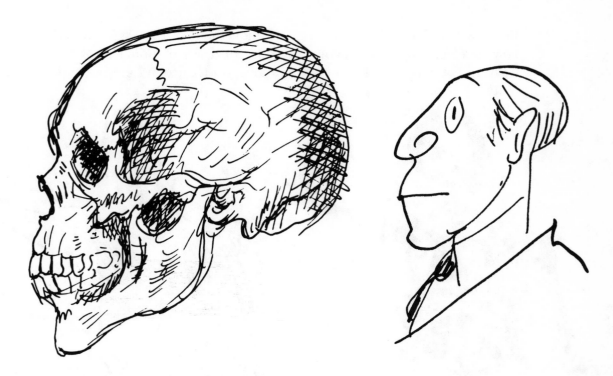

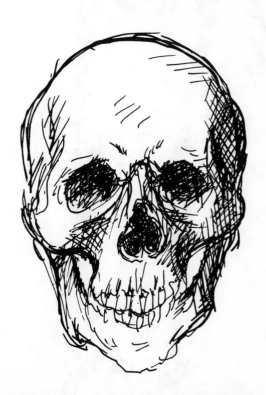

Know the human skull well, and it becomes much easier to draw a face. You will see the bones of the face protrude and the skull come through as if you were looking at an x-ray of the head.

Become familiar with the feeling and movement of the skeleton and how it affects the figures you are going to draw. Familiarity of the ways and actions of the skeleton will give your cartoon figures credibility.

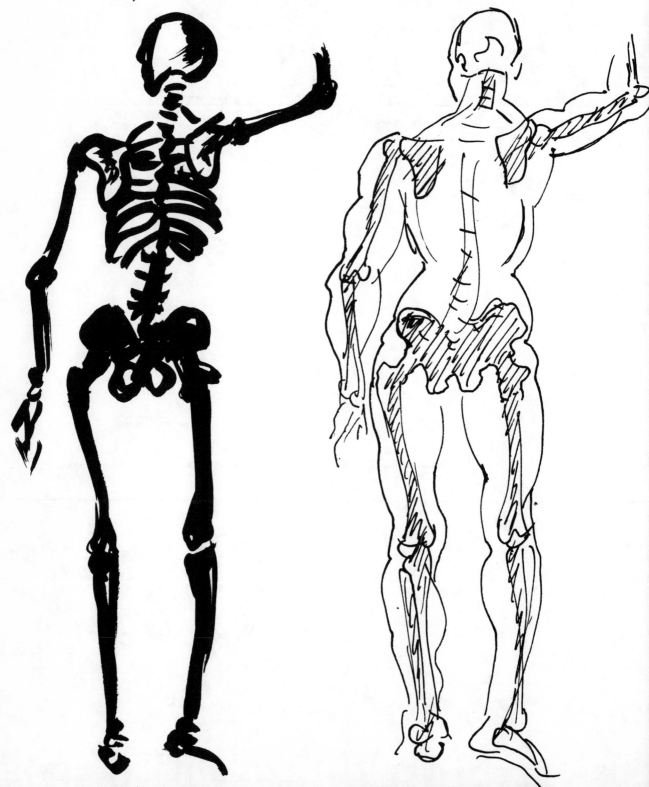

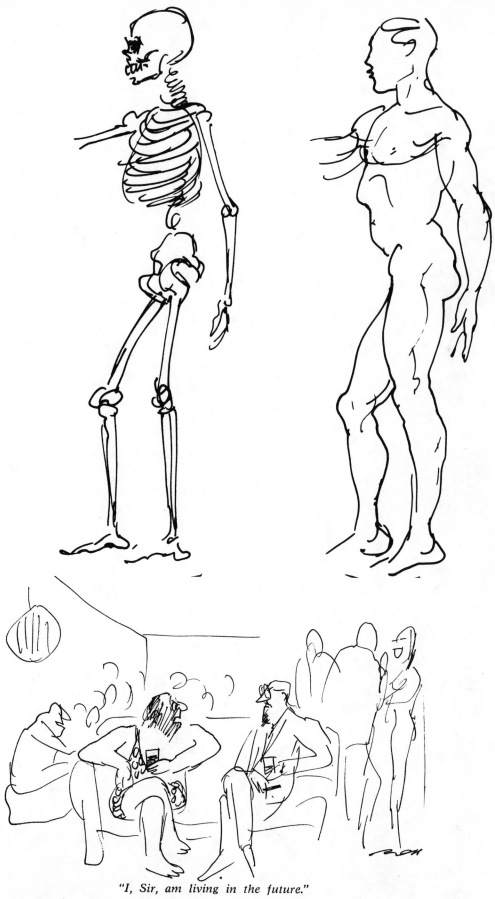

"I, Sir, am living in the future."

"Throw a few crumbs to one of them, and look what happens! They all want a few crumbs."

New Yorker, 1971

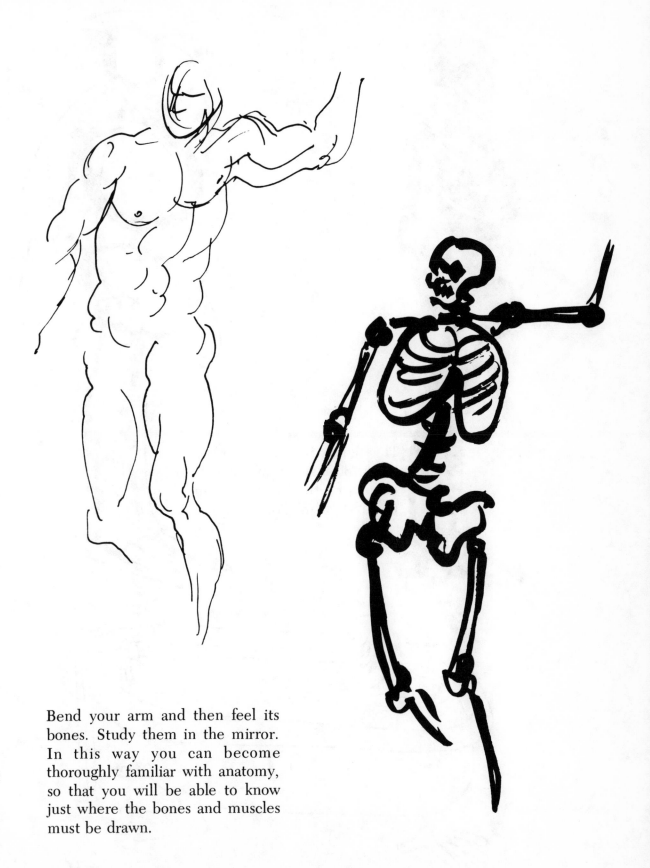

Bend your arm and then feel its bones. Study them in the mirror. In this way you can become thoroughly familiar with anatomy, so that you will be able to know just where the bones and muscles must be drawn.

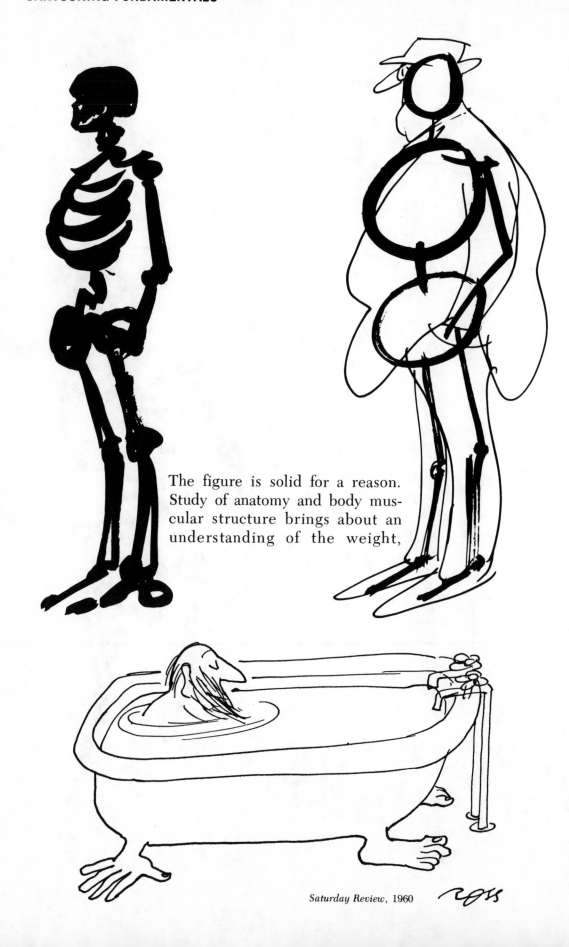

The figure is solid for a reason. Study of anatomy and body muscular structure brings about an understanding of the weight,

Saturday Review, 1960

shape, and form of the individual you draw, even when drawn in a quick and sketchy manner.

The torso, which is the nucleus of the body, has three major masses or divisions: the chest and rib cage at the top, the pelvic area at the bottom, and the soft mass of the belly between them. These masses are symmetrical, and they hang from an axis, which is the spine.

"That's the Stone Age for you."
New Yorker, 1974

The spine indicates the body's actions. The spine connects the head and neck, the upper torso, and the pelvic region. It is the central axis of the core of the body. It reacts to shifts of balance caused by the arms or legs.

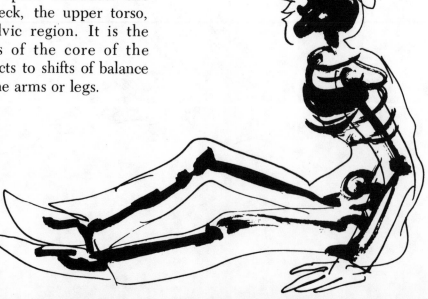

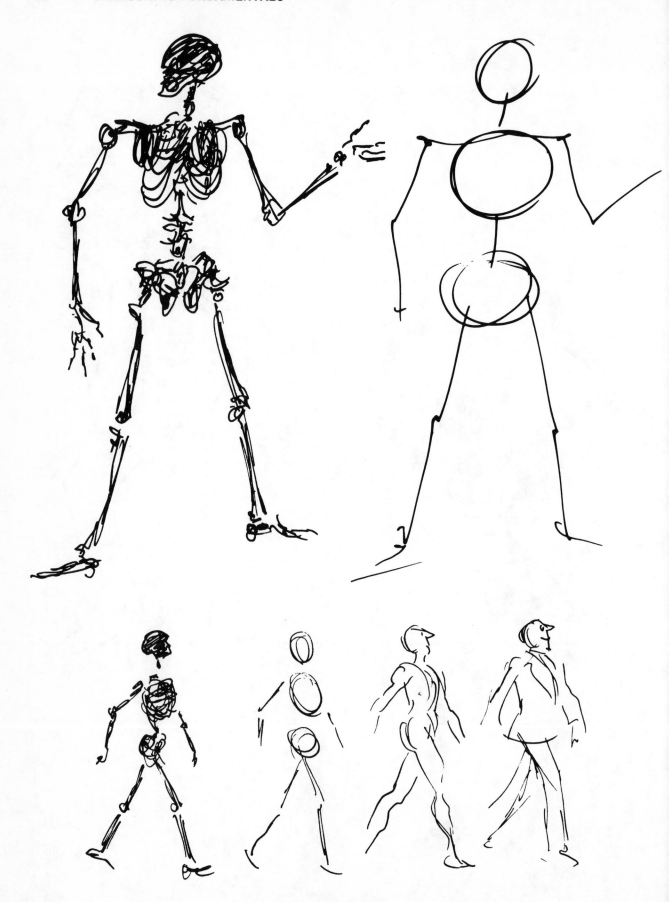

There need be only one or two steps between the doodle of a skeleton and the finished cartoon, as a study of this and the facing page clearly demonstrates. Notice how the detail has been kept to a minimum.

"Is this the 'R' part?"

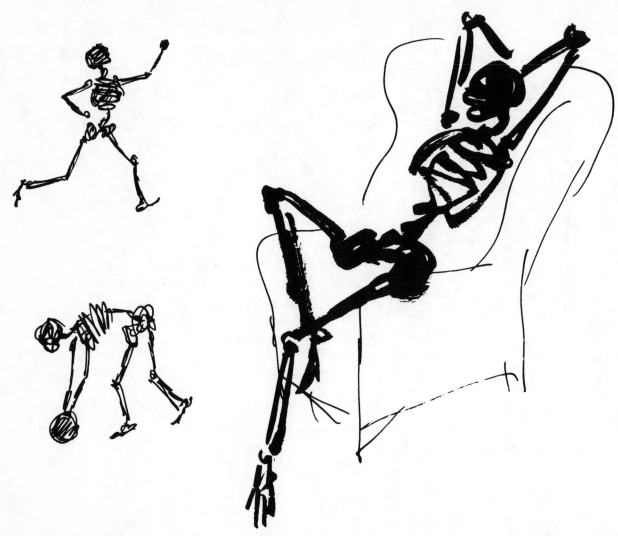

Skeleton doodling can be a lot of fun, and at the same time it will familiarize you with the very important underlying structure of the figure. After you have done plenty of this kind of doodling, you will be able to become very free and inventive.

DOODLING AND IMAGINATIVE DRAWINGS

Doodling is a great help to the budding cartoonist. It was for me, anyway. Doodling is thinking out loud on drawing paper with pen or pencil in hand. It sets the imagination free.

Many of the drawings that come through are subconscious; therefore, at times, doodling produces strange images. Through doodling and imaginative drawings I have evoked some of my most interesting characters.

Doodles are ideas in graphic form. They can lead to more studied forms of graphics. A lot of my doodles were developed later into larger drawings and eventually into paintings.

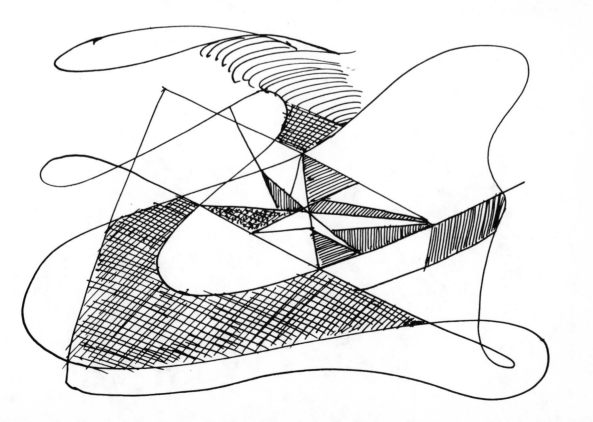

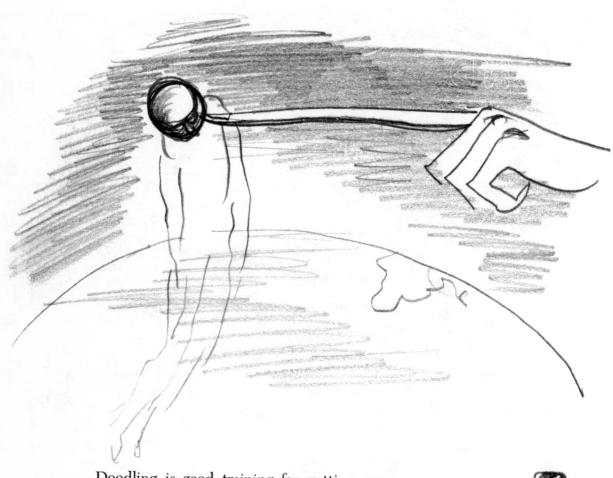

Doodling is good training for getting movement and freedom of expression into drawings and cartoons.

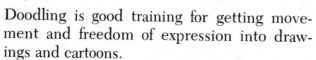

This is one of a series of forty doodles on the idea of a bird, created during a meeting with some fellow cartoonists.

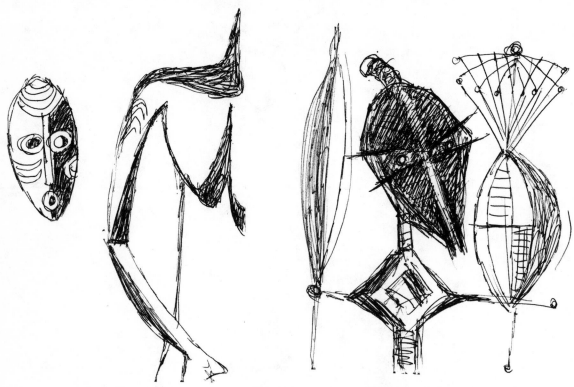

Doodling releases the imagination. There are no inhibitions, or pressures on the artist that might restrict his creative talent.

Watching the 1960 Olympics inspired the above doodles.

Abstract, surrealism, or pick-your-own school, doodling provides an opportunity to try your hand at any art form.

Doodling can take place anywhere and any-
time. You use whatever paper or cardboard
or envelope is at hand.

A conscious or semiconscious observation of most anything may become the germ of an idea, and cause you to begin to draw. Thus the doodle occurs.

Doodle on anything available. To the right is one I did on an envelope. Notice that the postmark and addressee's name are still legible. I just doodled right over them.

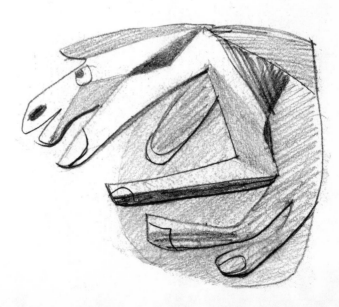

The doodles on this page subsequently inspired
two of my favorite oil paintings.

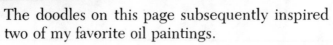

SKETCHING

SKETCHING, indoors or outdoors, is an essential exercise for developing skill in drawing. Try to carry odd-size sketchbooks for different occasions and locales.

Through constant sketching you enrich your collection of people—strange, beautiful, or whatever. They linger in your memory. Eventually they appear as performers in your cartoons.

Here are four wonderful faces, full of character caught in moments
of relaxation.

Sketching in such public places as trains and buses not only helps you to observe movement and attire of people, but it also gives you an insight into the character of people, which will eventually come through in your cartooning.

Different variations of the same young woman observed while sketching on a New York City subway. Each change of mood created a new basis for a sketch. I sketched her to the point of caricature.

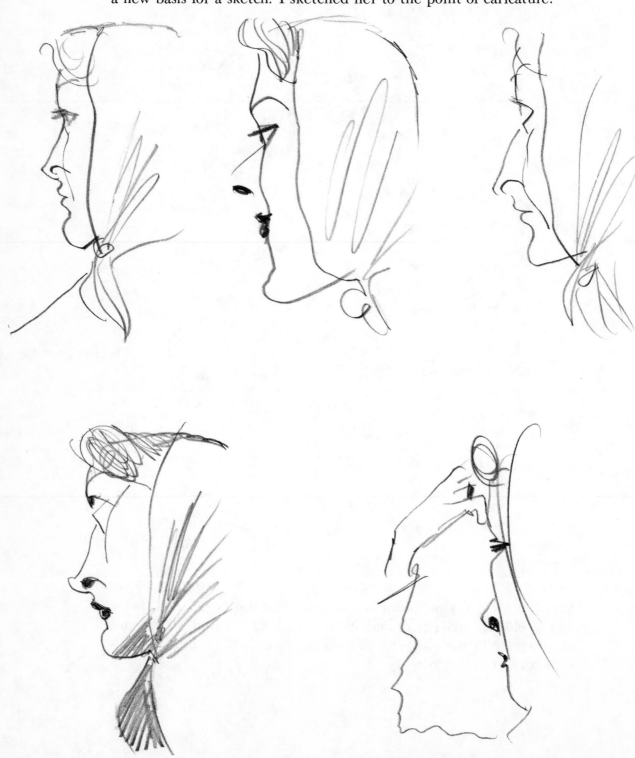

Once you get into the habit of sketching, you will find that the living outside world will be your studio. It is good for a student in an art-school classroom to find alternatives from the atmosphere of professional and posed models and to experience the outside world.

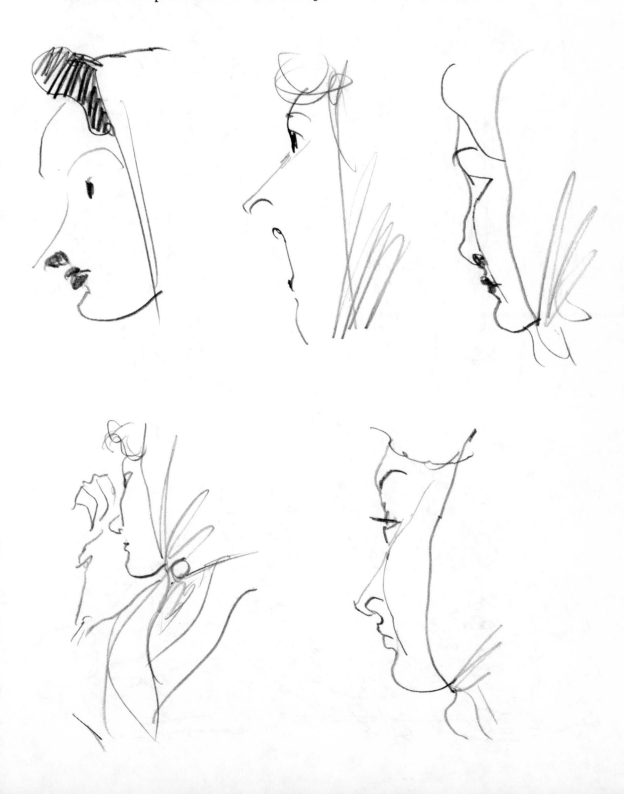

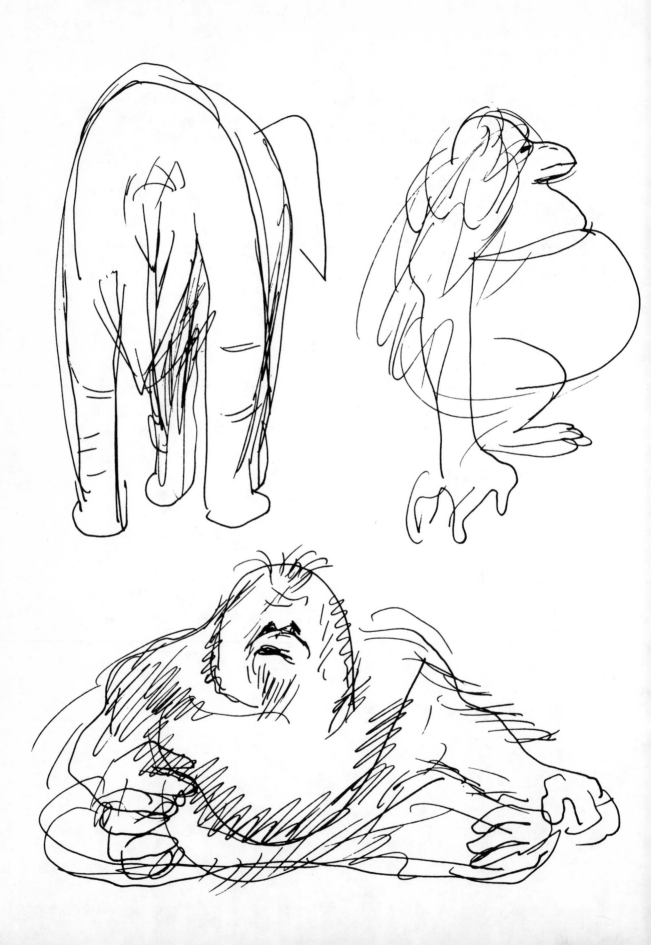

Sketching in the zoo is educational and a lot of fun. Keep drawing as the animal moves. As you watch the animal you will become familiar with the rhythm, the flow, the powerful movement of the body.

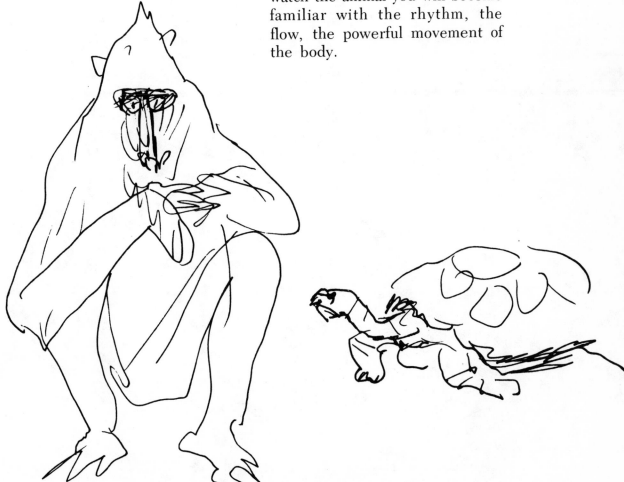

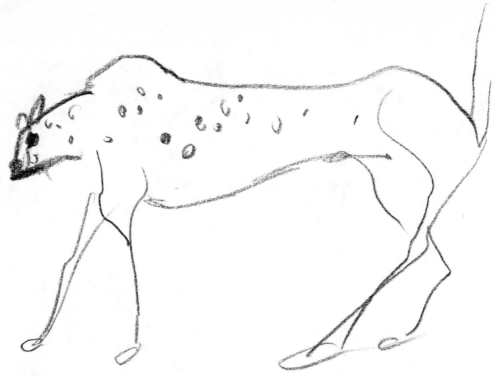

Various cats caught at the zoo around feeding time.

"What's happened to you? You used to enjoy
running with the pack."

New Yorker, 1967

"Not macaroni and cheese again!"

New Yorker, 1972

Sketches of people unaware that they were being observed and
characterized to the point of the cartoon.

Sketching from photographs is another way of exercising your drawing power.

Here are some observations of Pablo Picasso with friends and family I sketched from pictures in a French book on the great master.

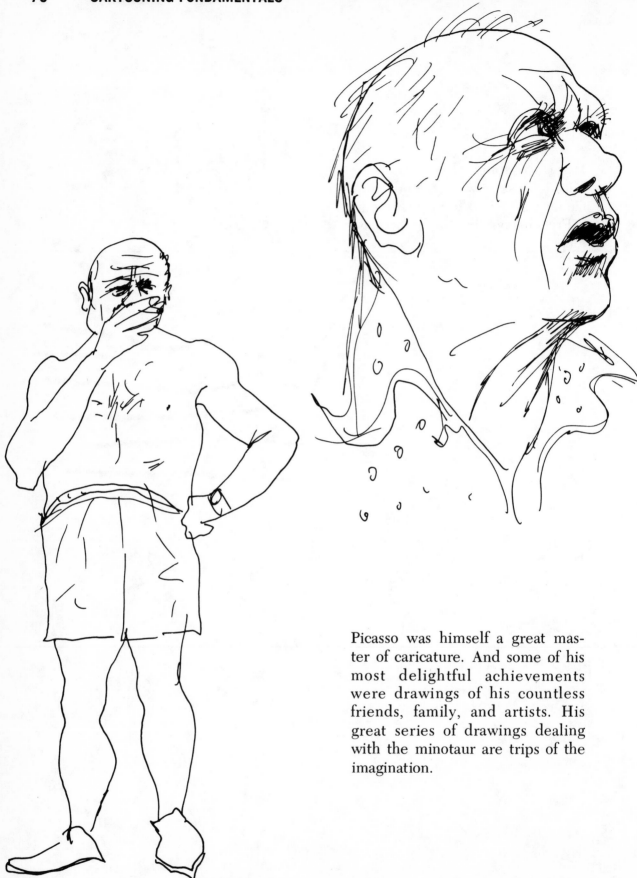

Picasso was himself a great master of caricature. And some of his most delightful achievements were drawings of his countless friends, family, and artists. His great series of drawings dealing with the minotaur are trips of the imagination.

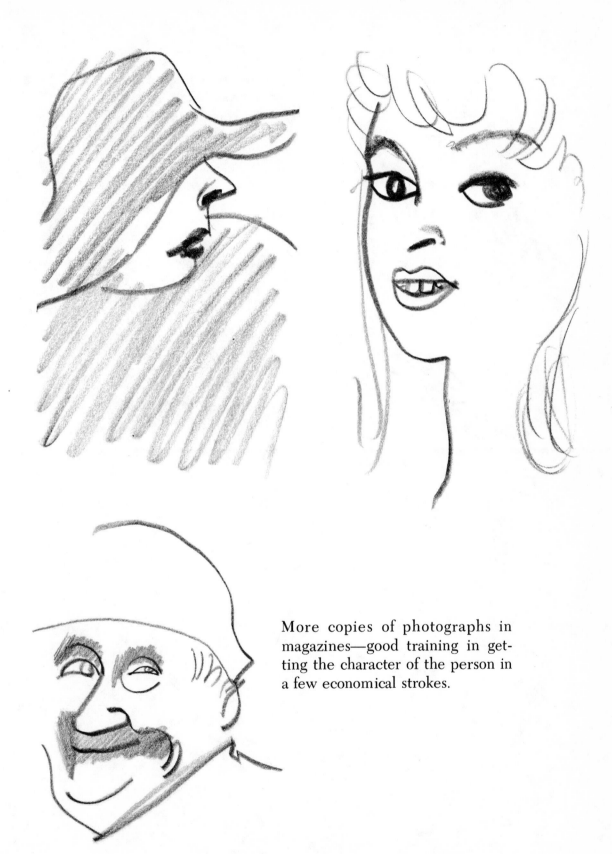

More copies of photographs in magazines—good training in getting the character of the person in a few economical strokes.

Here are some sketches I did while watching a television movie of the Napoleonic times.

FROM THE SKETCH TO THE CARTOON

FACES

As you continue to sketch, you will produce an endless array of faces. The faces of countless people that you observed without sketching will be retained deep inside of you, and will appear as the faces in your cartoon characters. A certain kind of face and expression will probably appeal to you and may even be associated with your own physiognomy and character.

The most valuable asset a cartoonist can have is the ability to experiment until he has discovered new approaches in creating heads and
figures. Be aware of the infinite variety of differences in detail as
you observe the people around you. In your drawings you can caricature at will all these varieties of eyes, noses, mouths, ears, and
hairlines.

Faces come with expressions. Expressions are endless. If you just look in the mirror, you can create a great many of your own.

The faces of the husband and wife in this cartoon have just the right expression to convey the idea. The more slapstick the more the facial expressions are exaggerated.

"Sometimes I think all the bank cares about is money!"

SATURDAY REVIEW, 1969

"Dad, I've been experimenting with life."

Saturday Review, 1971

All kids are cute, and there's an endless variety of them. After a while you will notice that a certain type will continually appear in your cartoons.

ACTION

Action, they say, speaks louder than words. Certainly, in cartooning, the idea must always be indicated by the proper action. In fact one of the features that causes a drawing to become a cartoon is the creation of humor by exaggerating the action.

Above: Women at a sale offer a cartoonist a subject with plenty of action. *Below:* This gesture—one arm up and one arm down—is loaded with action.

Left: The man jumping across a puddle combines the appropriate action, with the expression to go with the situation. *Below:* The action of the woman at the washtub is the essence of this cartoon sequence.

The rhythm of give and take is the central action in a prize-fight. Observe that whenever the right arm goes forward, the right leg goes backward. The same combination is demonstrated in the walking man, *below*.

"He's the seventeenth Earl of Wexford. The other sixteen were just as bad."

Saturday Review, 1970

Below: A sense of action results from the movement created by the angle of the woman's body as she bends over, with hands on hips, and the complementary tilt of the man's head. The man's crossed legs add to the movement of the entire picture.

Above: Lively street action, with pedestrians facing opposite ways
Below: A couple of guys having a laugh over a beer

Full follow-through action on
the part of the football player

The backward flip of the two
dancers' legs gives a strong feeling
of rhythm.

THE CARTOON CHARACTER

All the people you come in contact with in everyday life provide possible characters for cartoons. Include not only the people you see in the flesh, but those you see on stage, screen, television, and also the people of your imagination. Here are some I saw or dreamed up.

A burglar, on his way to work

An average citizen, reflecting on what he saw in his newspaper

A cop, with his eye on the burglar

A penny for her thoughts!

One

Three

Fifteen

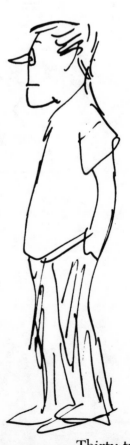

Thirty-two

Eight

Fourteen

Fifty-eight

Seventy-five

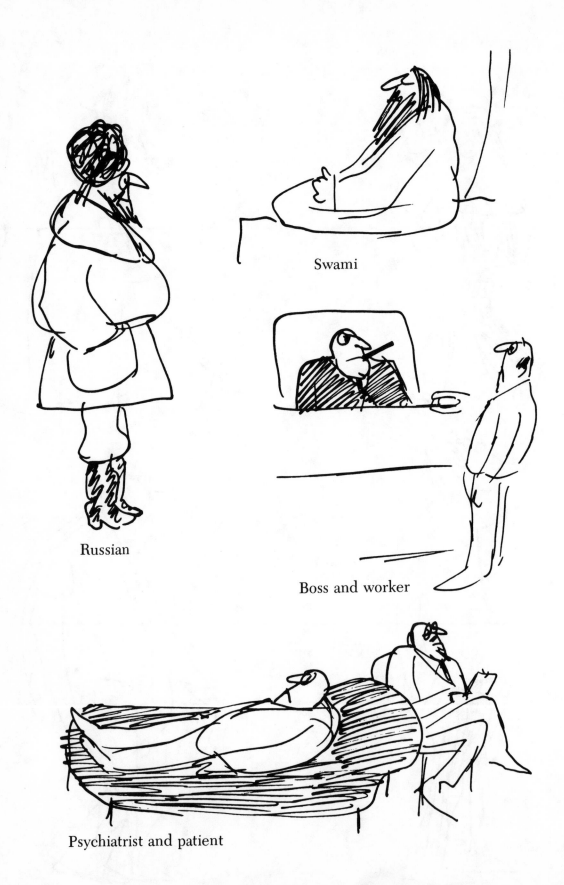

Russian

Swami

Boss and worker

Psychiatrist and patient

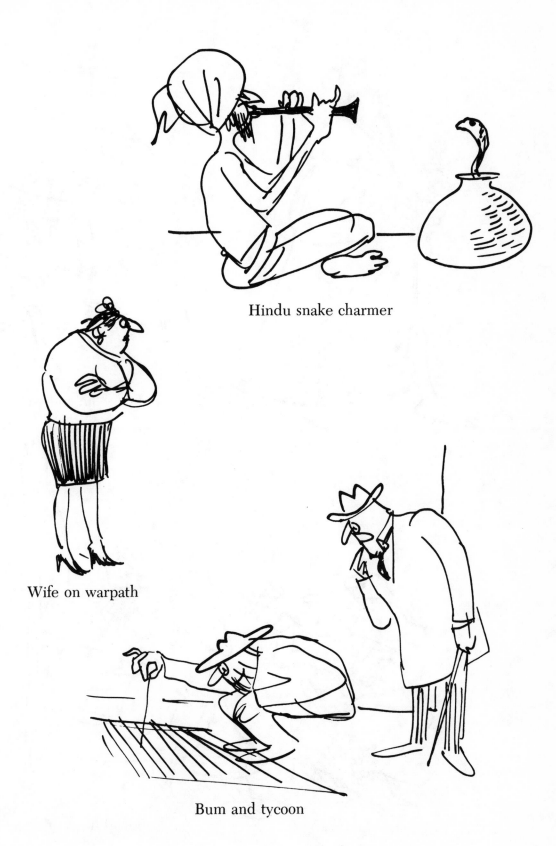

Hindu snake charmer

Wife on warpath

Bum and tycoon

King

Boy scout and old lady

King and his jester

Drunk

Old man and little girl

The Old Year - and the New

Jailbird

Uncle Sam

WATCH OUT!

Soothsayer

Man and his dog

Businessman

Pals

Artist

Cowboy

Indian

Baseball player

TEXTURE

Texture gives life to your dressed-up cartoon characters. It also adds sparkle and body to your over-all cartoon design.

Lady with a fur jacket

The boss in a snappy striped suit

Girl on couch in a shiny dress

Man in black suit with pin stripes
(created by scratching on black
area with a razor blade)

Girl in wool cap and sweater outfit

Old boy in tweed jacket,
turtleneck sweater, and checked
slacks

Swami and his mystic robe

Stone-age man and animal suit

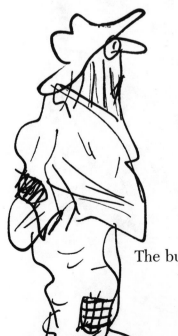

The bum and his rags

Sleepy lady in bathrobe and nightgown

REPENT NOW! AVOID THE RUSH ON DOOMSDAY!

AL ROSS

LOOK, 1963

Train engineer and outfit

Lady in dress with flower design

Swordsman of the fifteenth century, ready for an encounter with the enemy

Checks on the chair and a touch of a small pattern on the drapes lends color to the picture.

A variety or textures are to be found in the street. Keep a sharp lookout for these when sketching outdoors. Make notations and file them away—they will prove useful when creating pictures.

HANDS

The hands play an important part in portraying attitudes and gestures in cartoons. Here are a group of hands copied from the masters. The hand in the upper-righthand corner is by the great nineteenth-century Japanese painter Hokusai. Note the split-second movements of the fingers. The others are by Michelangelo and his German contemporary, Mathias Grünewald.

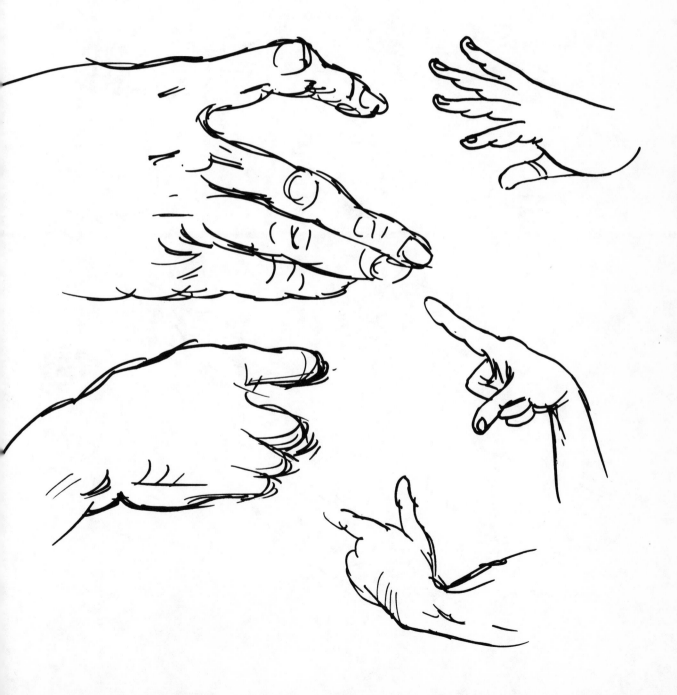

Most beginners in cartooning have difficulty in drawing hands. Some simply avoid the problem by putting the character's hands in his pocket, or behind his back. A badly drawn hand in its proper place, however, is far better than a hidden hand.

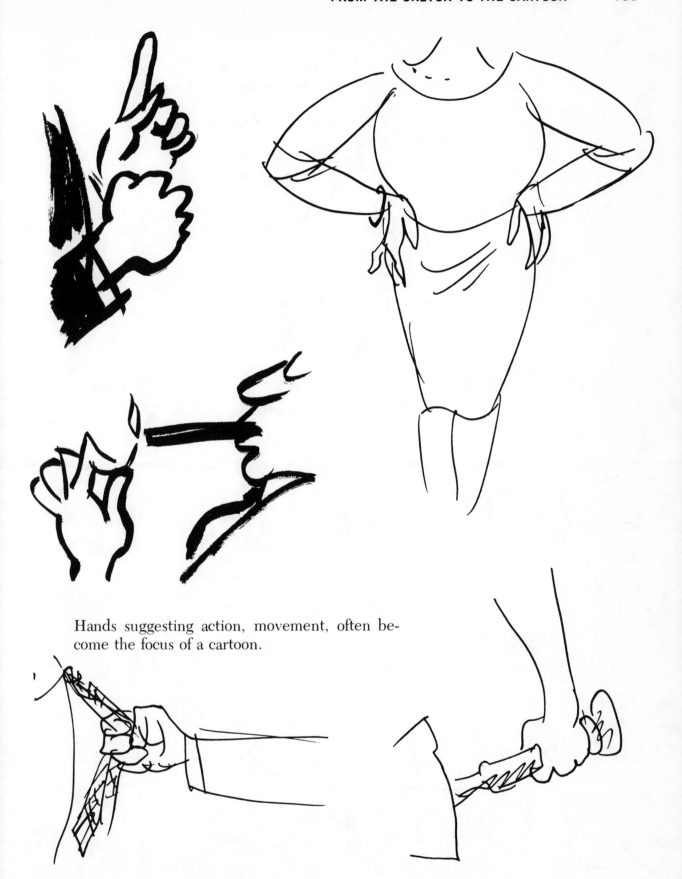

Hands suggesting action, movement, often become the focus of a cartoon.

It is not necessary to construct anatomically perfect hands in a cartoon. However, all drawings of hands must follow certain rules in order to be acceptable. Hands are sometimes just as important as facial expressions in a pose.

LIGHT AND SHADE

As you advance to attempting a variety of cartoon techniques, you will find it useful to create in wash and ben day. Both of these mediums require a knowledge of shading, that is, drawing people and things in light and shade. You will want to illustrate your cartoons simply, suggesting light and shade by the most obvious means. You will not need to suggest subtle variations of shadow such as fine artists must learn.

Notice the way light falls on objects around you. For example: Set up a small box under a strong light. Notice how the light illuminates one side brightly and throws the other side into shadow. Study the

examples of shading on these two pages. In the section below on my various cartoon styles you will see ways in which I have dealt with light and shadow in greater depth.

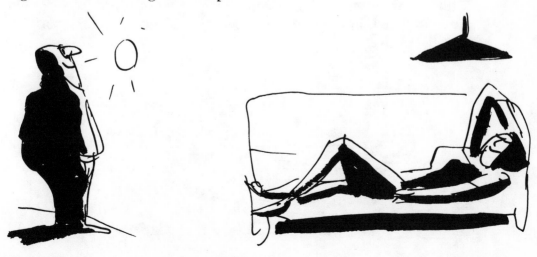

The strong use of light and shade can lend drama to a picture and can help to create a more powerful design. In this cartoon the shadow falling on the judge's bench repeats the action of the lawyer, bringing more movement and tension into the picture. This is just one example of what can be done with light and shade.

In the drawing on the left shading gives solidity to the picture. On the other hand, in the *New Yorker* cartoon, shading is used sparingly but effectively.

A good example of shading using wash on a cartoon which I did in 1947. The wash is applied with the same bravura that is applied to the manipulation of the brush drawing.

"Stop it! Have you both forgotten that you volunteered as non-combatants?"

WRINKLES

A close study of people in clothes and in action will reveal the relationship between the solid form underneath and the wrinkles created during movement.

Include only the important wrinkles, and try not to overload your drawing with a lot of scratchy lines.

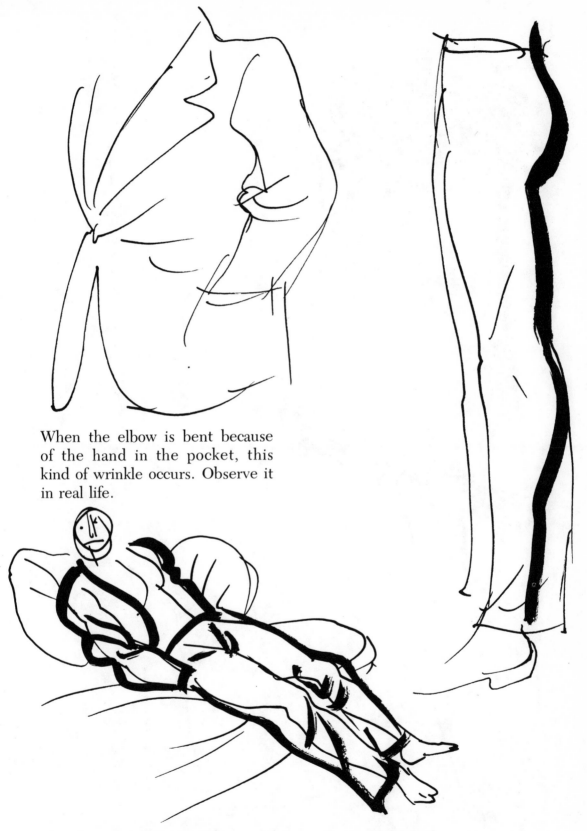

When the elbow is bent because of the hand in the pocket, this kind of wrinkle occurs. Observe it in real life.

Note how the clothing drapes over the contours of the body.

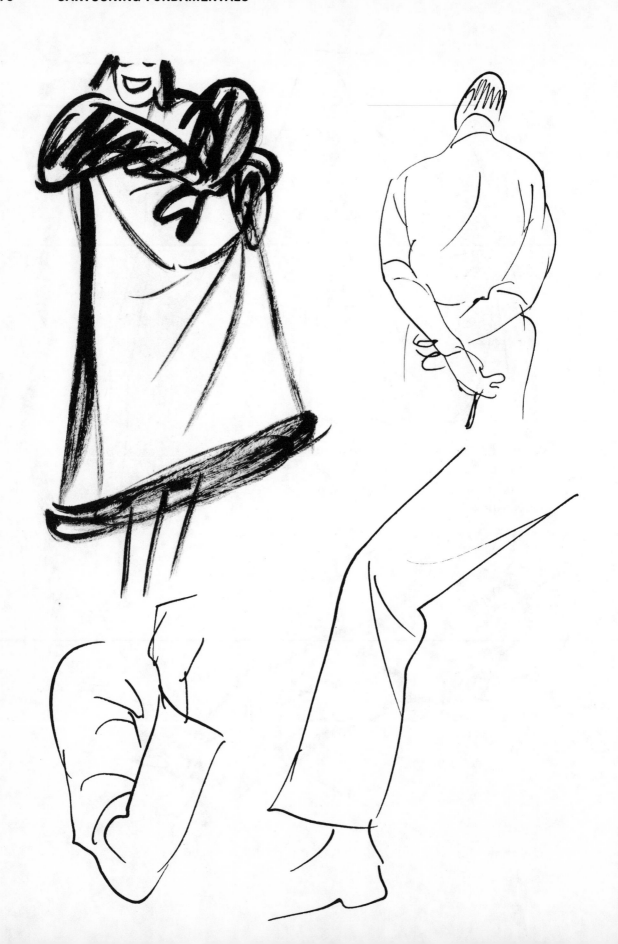

The thigh is revealed here by a few wrinkles in the right places.

Wrinkles, resulting from action, flow with the
mood of the scene. In these drawings there is
just enough to get the feel of action in the clothing. Too many wrinkles will spoil the picture.

EENY

MEENY

MINEY

MO

STYLES AND TECHNIQUES

IN THE THIRTIES, my style of cartooning was devoted mainly to shading and modeling with a conté pencil. I liked the medium and it gave me a lot of opportunities to create light and shade. Details were precise and I was able to arrive at fine gradations of tone. It was, of course, a somewhat illustrative style of cartooning.

"I thought I fired you, Miss Spleen!"

"I suppose you both want the same thing?"

"New on the force, ain't you, son?"

"Hello, dear—Look, homework!"

Later on, my perpetual drawing from the model and sketching at every opportunity led me to discard the all-pencil technique and use wash with a more sketchy handling of the pencil outline. This technique gave me more freedom in creating movement in the handling of my cartoon characters—and they became quite a bunch of characters!

"Have you a recording of Beethoven's Silly Symphony?"

A. ROSS

" . . . In this corner, Babe Thompson!"

I then began to use black areas in my designs to give solidity to the picture and to create an over-all strong pictorial look. My style, however, was still an illustrative cartoon style.

"Here's your change, buddy."

"Mother warned me it wouldn't
be safe to go driving with you!"

In the forties my style became more animated as my line developed.
I used brush with ink or wash. This again was the result of my
sketching, which was now being done in direct use of brush. My
characters became more humorous and less studied and illustrative.
Even my sense of humor was more alive.

"Better pull down your shade, Miss Wilmot,
we'll be flying over Mt. Wilson Observatory soon."

"Now that we're divorced,
the least you can do is
give me my old job back!"

COLLIER'S   AL ROSS

Again, the strong use of blacks and the sure handling of the brush with india-ink produced interesting patterns of design, creating a good-looking picture.

COLLIER'S   "The cad caught me out with his wife!"   AL ROSS

The gradations of wash tones create an interesting design. The brush line is fast and spontaneous. This technique became highly developed in the fifties, when I created and sold a great many cartoons. I also was able to acquire many jobs of illustrating humorous stories and articles.

THE SATURDAY EVENING POST

"Do you happen to have a bottle of glue handy?"

Another example of my high point of development of the style of the fifties. Wash and line are free-flowing. The signature, you will note, has become more fluid.

"My son handles the present."

"I'm not goofing off. It so happens that the mind paints before the brush!"

Country Beautiful, 1965

"I, for one, do not intend to surrender to facts!"

In the sixties, I began to use pen-line and wash. The people became zanier and funnier. The handling of the figures and surroundings became more humorous. I discovered the great fluid use of the pen, which became easier to handle than the brush. Wash was used differently from the way it was used with the brush style; it became less an element of pattern and more flowing and lighter.

"Where did you get the penny?"

Saturday Review, 1969

In the late sixties and into the seventies, pure line became my expression. I abandoned wash. Tone and nuance were accomplished by the action of the pen. The drawings were produced spontaneously in a hit-or-miss fashion. There were no pencil outlines of the figures before I used the pen. Sometimes four or five drawings were made before the execution and composition satisfied me, sometimes it took only one drawing to get what I was after.

"In my third reincarnation, we were rather well-to-do."
New Yorker, 1968

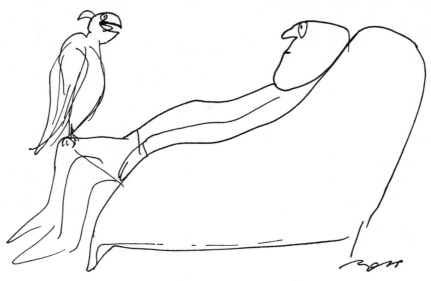

"Talk to me."

Saturday Review, 1972

"I like this stream. There's no dirt backwash!"

New Yorker, 1968

"In fourteen hundred and ninety-two, you will sail the ocean blue."

New Yorker, 1971

New Yorker, 1974

World, 1972

New Yorker, 1974

COPYING THE MASTERS

I still copy and draw from the masters. On this page is a copy of a Rembrandt and two copies of works by Georges Rouault. These are just samples of hundreds of drawings of famous masters I copied to formulate my own style of expression.

Edgar Degas was a master draftsman. His wonderful handling of the figure always fascinated me. His expressions of movement in the drawings of his famous ballet dancers are beautifully handled and masterfully executed. I did countless copies of his dancers and portraits of people. Some of these copies are on this and on the facing page.

El Greco's figures always moved me greatly. His people were monumental and at times elongated to the point of caricature and cartoon. I copied a lot of them and did some improvising on my own. I felt a stimulating surge to use the pen boldly when I looked at his art.

Honoré Daumier, a great painter and cartoonist, influenced many artists, including Peter Arno, John Groth and Whitney Darrow, Jr. He created wonderful characters in his courtroom scenes. His compositions and his black, white and gray patterns continue to be a source of inspiration to me. On this and the facing page are copies I made of several of Daumier's works.

The bold black strokes of Georges Rouault are emotional, as are his people and subject matter. A long apprenticeship in the studio of Gustave Moreau inspired these grotesque cartoon-like characters. He also drew for inspiration on the genius of Rembrandt, Goya, and Daumier. On this and the facing page are copies I made of several of Rouault's drawings.

The powerful drawings and paintings of Rico Lebrun, with whom I studied at the Art Students League, were and remain a constant inspiration to me. His art is in the great Renaissance tradition. When Lebrun moved to California, he influenced many young artists on the West Coast. Above is a copy I made of a painting by Lebrun.

Harpo Marx

Jean Paul Belmondo

CARICATURE

Successful caricatures are possible because the artist has applied himself to the deliberate study of exaggeration. The word itself comes from the Italian *caricare*, which means to load or, figuratively, to exaggerate. Webster says, "caricature is a grotesque or ludicrous exaggeration of parts or characteristics." You, too, can draw caricatures if you train your eye to pick out the features in a face to exaggerate. Make sketches first. The best ones are combined to produce the finished product.

The first and most obvious step involves the head. Reduce the head to a simple shape. Next, observe which features are most prominent. The nose is usually the key to the placement of other features in a successful caricature. Emphasize the obvious. Use great care when drawing eyes and mouth. Make notes of important wrinkles. Study the weight of eyebrows. Combine all the elements in small preliminary sketches.

Jackie Gleason

Pope John XXIII

The ferociously expressive face of Russian Premier Aleksei Kosygin is characterized by exaggerating the strong dark eyes and scowl. The large forehead is made larger, the foxlike ears pointier. Bristling hair adds to the likeness.

The shape of the face of Martin Luther King, Jr., has to be established. His eyes are shown wide apart, and the rhythm of the nose, mustache, and mouth as one unit is stressed.

The famous outstanding nose of actor Jimmy Durante is, of course, greatly exaggerated. The small beady eyes add a strong contrast. The narrow face is brought out by pointing the chin. The eyebrows add to the Durante expression. Even the hat has to be caricatured.

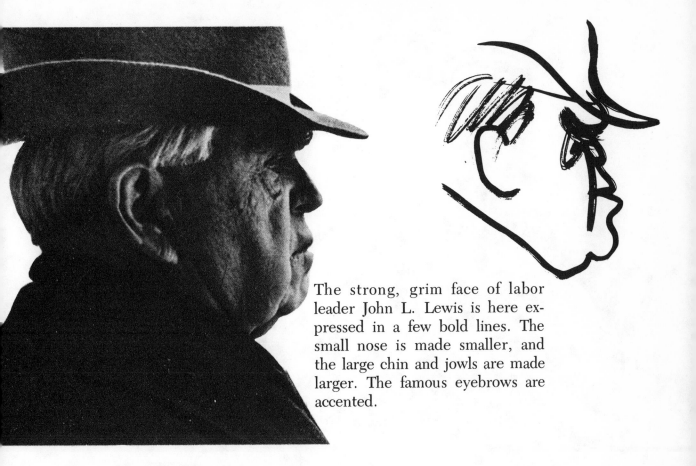

The strong, grim face of labor leader John L. Lewis is here expressed in a few bold lines. The small nose is made smaller, and the large chin and jowls are made larger. The famous eyebrows are accented.

The very expressive nose and mouth of Shirley Chisholm, Congresswoman from New York, are here exaggerated to bring out the full nature of the fiery legislator.

Make a ball for a nose, accent the mustache and laugh, pinch the little oval glasses and the narrowed eyes close together, and you have a caricature of Teddy Roosevelt. The particular shape of Teddy's head has to be established.

The famous smile of Dwight D. Eisenhower is accented to establish his personality. His large forehead has that "baby" look, an important feature. His eyes are strong, set apart, and exaggerated. Add a pointy nose and pointy chin.

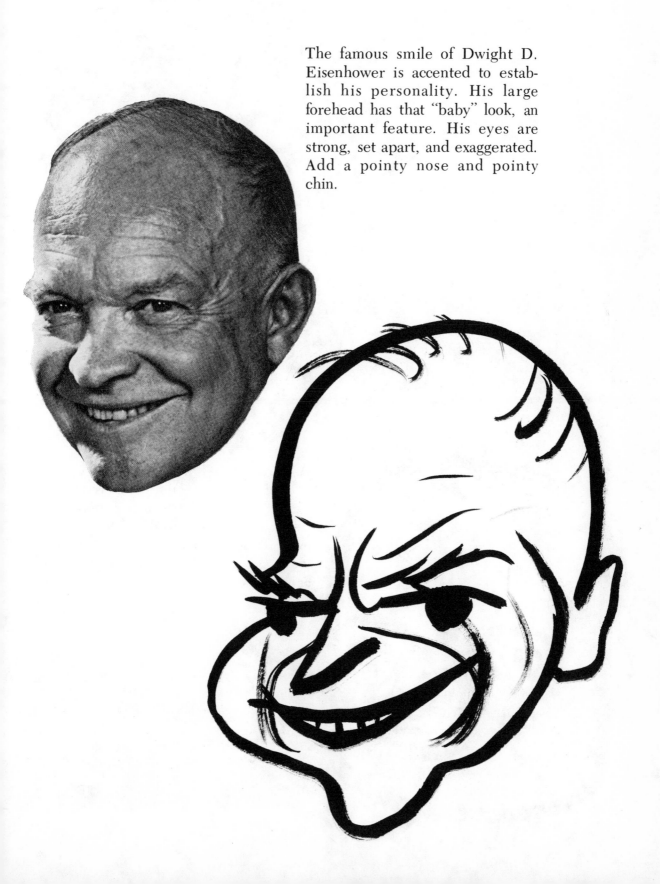

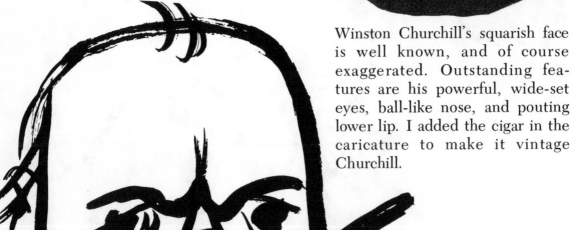

Winston Churchill's squarish face is well known, and of course exaggerated. Outstanding features are his powerful, wide-set eyes, ball-like nose, and pouting lower lip. I added the cigar in the caricature to make it vintage Churchill.

The calm, tolerant look, so characteristic of comedian Jack Benny, is well expressed in this photo. The smile is the key to the success of the caricature. The eyes peeking out through the glasses give that "Jack Benny" look.

In this caricature of Muhammad Ali, I accented the wide face and strong jaw. But, the key to the caricature is the nose. Once I established the character of the nose, the expressive mouth and his famous lower lip followed automatically.

Estaban Soriano was a great caricaturist, as well as a cartoonist and fine artist. He caricatured people constantly. This is a page of his caricatures created about 1945 at a meeting of a cartoonists organization. The author is at bottom right, then a young man with a lot of hair.

COMPOSITION

In looking at works of art, always search for the important lines and masses in the composition. Analyze it to get at the bottom of the basic rhythm of the work. In this way you acquire a sense of composition, which is of tremendous help to you, consciously and unconsciously, when you create your own drawings.

Note the outstanding "D" shape Rembrandt has created in this beautiful composition. The boy in the foreground is brought forward by the shadows on the other figures, making him the focal point from which the picture spreads out.

In this composition by George Rouault, note the importance of the two dark areas in the right back area. They hold the composition in place by establishing an equilibrium of the figures and the background.

Below: The beautiful rhythmic flow of the pen is the outstanding characteristic of this drawing by Picasso. The strong vertical structure of the figures is cleverly balanced by the horizontal areas in the background.

Just knowing how to draw funny characters in a skillful way is not enough to sell cartoons. Cartoon characters in themselves cannot illustrate an idea unless they are related to an appropriate setting. The art of placing characters in a drawing, or "staging," is, of course, an element of composition. You must learn to put your characters in the right place and then direct the reader's eye to the leading figure that brings out the cartoon idea—which is, in most cases, the person talking. It is thus very important that you study how to place the positive emphasis in each picture you compose.

Imagine your drawing as if it were a stage set. The director in a play takes a lot of time in arranging the background of the set to make it appear more convincing to the audience. Unless he can make the audience believe the scene, the effect of the characters may be lost. Similarly, if an editor, who is "auditing" a cartoon, spots an amateurish presentation in it, he will be more likely to reject it. When you set the stage for your drawing, whether it be a rough sketch or a finished drawing, follow these rules:

1. Every drawing should have a center of interest.
2. Every drawing should include authentic background.
3. Every drawing should show a knowledge of perspective.

"I'm all for equal rights, but that's going <u>too</u> far!"

Note the simplicity and compact appearance of this composition. The center of interest is the woman kicking the car, but you quickly notice the man talking and then the eye shoots back again to the woman and the action. By placing the pole on the left, the rhythm of the picture moves in a slight bottom arch from left to right, creating an interesting design. Note the strong feeling of perspective.

"No 'Ho-ho-ho' at all, Mr. Reynolds, is better than a 'Ho-ho-ho' that doesn't come from the heart."

In this composition the center of interest is Santa Claus. The eye sets on Santa and the kids, and then moves to the Manager, who is doing the talking. The column in back of him serves as a strong upright shape to hold the right side of the composition, and also to create depth—as do the children on the left, and the Christmas tree. The Manager, leaning into the picture, creates a counter-action to the line on the left created by the kids and the left part of the tree, thus adding to the action and making an interesting positive design.

The droopy attitude of the woman and the counter-attitude of the man make this a strong composition. The black areas are well balanced.

"I think I'll enter you in the dog show."

1,000 Jokes, *DELL PUB.*

Here the portrayal of the main character in the picture is brought to a more dramatic impact by the tree behind him. The tree also connects him to the couple in the background, and moreover creates a sense of depth. To add a picture on the wall or more than a hint of furniture would have upset the delicate balance of the composition.

"I think he hates Agnew most, then George Wallace—then me."

NEW YORKER, 1970

"Come on out, Blackie! We know you're in there!"

The tree is the main "character" here. The police car provides important shape in the right spot for balance. Buildings form a strong background. Little policemen create the action. Wash tones, carefully weighed, supply additional interesting shape to the composition.

The curve in the road makes this an interesting composition, and also gives a feeling of depth to the succession of cars. The woman's face and the sign are carefully placed.

Above: The composition is bad because it allows too much space between the principal figures in the picture. Moreover, it provides a space above them that immediately involves the eye. Even if a few figures were inserted in the space, the composition would still be bad.

Below: Here the composition is greatly improved. Everything is more compact, with no gaping openings to distract from the main characters. The space above them is just enough to give breathing air and movement to the scale of the picture.

"Your wife's on the phone. The azaleas are out."

The problem of composing a table full of people was solved by bunching them, in proper perspective, on one side of the picture. The person talking is the link connecting the boss and the rest of the people into a unit. He stands out as the one talking, at the same time giving action to the picture.

"Darling, I'd like to have you meet Quigley, Quigley, Hemsworth and Farrell."

The spacing of the characters is very important in this cartoon composition. The four gentlemen are bunched together in one segment. Had they been closer, the message of the cartoon would not have come across as effectively. The tones give the picture weight. Had I added more tone to the husband, the four men would have had to be treated similarly, thus creating an entirely different picture and problem.

CARTOON ILLUSTRATION

A SEQUENCE OF ILLUSTRATIONS to the text of an industrial magazine teach safety to company employees.

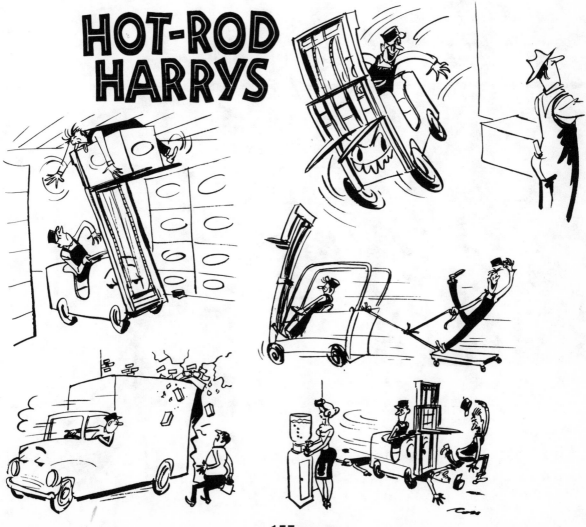

Left: Illustrations for an article dealing with the way "the finance man sees your failures." In the article, each cause of failures is discussed in about one hundred words, which include the key line or sentence that appears below each drawing. My task was to provide a humorous graphic comment to suit the key lines.

Below: In this illustration, my job was to add to the mystery of the man punching the clock, who is the "silent stool pigeon" in the story.

YOU BE THE ARBITRATOR

THE CASE OF

The silent stool pigeon

Out of the experience of the American Arbitration Association

These fashion drawings for a children's magazine were done from photos of the various clothes. I gave it a lot of action by animating the kids, and keeping the whole thing in a sketchy manner. This is what the editor wanted. The intention was to eliminate the usual dull feeling of fashion design.

For bed, beach or everyday activity even in the back yard

E.. is 'everyhour' fashion

"Say You Saw it in INFANTS' & CHILDREN'S REVIEW for February, 1965"

These spot illustrations appeared in the monthly *Factory* magazine, published by the McGraw-Hill Publishing Co. The editor would supply me with tear-sheets of the text to be illustrated.

HUMAN RELATIONS
By V. E. LUNARDI, Assistant Editor, FACTORY

Interviewer ferrets out facts

Clerks on salary elevator

This story for *Factory* asked for a more serious kind of illustration. The concept was comparatively easy to acquire. The main problems were the composition and creating the characters. By bringing Michele Savarino, the main character, conspicuously into the foreground, I was able to establish a strong composition and at the same time bring out the colorful character of his face.

"Foreman say you fired."

The
Mad Butcher
of
Queensbury
Run
3

Two illustrations show two different techniques used in book and magazine illustrations. In one, the simple use of pen, ink, and brush created a pleasing pattern of gray and black. In the other (below), pencil, wash, and smudging of the pencil over the wash, to create a pleasing tonality which, of course, coincided with the idea behind the illustration.

Factory, McGraw-Hill

I fear thy kisses, gentle maiden.
                    —Percy Bysshe Shelley

Here we have illustrations spontaneously
created as I depicted the love story of girl
and boy from childhood to maturity. All in
line, it was hit or miss. If I missed, I tried
again and again until I got the free-flowing
expression I was after.

Using a simple technique of line and wash, I created over one hundred cartoon illustrations for a humorous book on bridge and gin. I had free rein, and the book was greatly enhanced by the many zany characters who take bridge and gin seriously.

Big-Mouth Snapper Pigeon

Timid Tippy-Toe Pigeon

Broken-Friendship Trick

Friendly Homing Pigeon

Irritation Ploy

CREATING CARTOON IDEAS

Everyone tells you that you have a great sense of humor. You're learning to draw cartoons, and you're always looking for ideas. There are several ways of getting ideas for cartoons.

One way is to be constantly alert and aware of your surroundings, and of people around you. As you progress with your cartooning, you will develop a "gag-mind"—you will spontaneously try to find an idea in anything you observe in the street, or wherever you note anything peculiar or out of the ordinary happening.

In other words, your mind becomes like a seismograph, very sensitive to anything you see or to whatever occurs around you. Also, you will develop a sharp ear. You will pick up phrases or remarks that you hear at random. These will quickly be turned into cartoon ideas by your mind. You will be very alert to associations, such as a remark someone just made or some other action happening around the same time.

In your studio, another way of creating ideas is to thumb through magazines. After a while the pictures, ads, and other features will tap your imagination. There is a certain resistance you must break through, and when that happens the ideas begin to come. Thumbing through cartoon books will also give you ideas.

Another way to approach idea making is to choose one subject and create as many variations on it as you can. Chances are you will pull two or three out that have strong selling ability.

After a while, your own particular sense of humor will emerge and you will display your own point of view. This is highly creative cartooning. An example of this kind of cartooning is that of George Price of *The New Yorker*, who has a superb sense of humor, and the people in his cartoons are real.

If you have trouble creating ideas, you can buy them from very gifted gag-writers, including those who advertise in the *Writers Digest*. You can choose the ideas that suit your particular sense of humor and your cartoon style. Even if the ideas come from someone else, you can give them your interpretation and rendering, which will make them your very own.

"Now that you ask, I'm damned if I do know what 'oyez' means!"
New Yorker, 1975

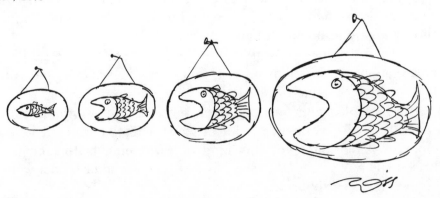

THE CARTOON ROUGH

THE MOST IMPORTANT THING about the cartoon rough is clarity in expressing the idea. When you submit your rough to the editor, if the idea doesn't hit him quickly, he will just pass it on. Do the rough sketch over and over until you clearly express what you're trying to say. It doesn't matter how sketchy the rough is, as long as the editor gets the idea. Also make sure that the caption of the cartoon, if there is one, is clearly lettered. Backgrounds should be simple and rough. In the finished drawing you can be more explicit in your detail.

On this and the facing page are roughs exactly as I submitted them to cartoon editors. Notice that I have hand-lettered the captions on the cartoons. Unfortunately, I can't show you published cartoons of these roughs, because at this moment I have had only rejection slips, which proves a point: no matter how long, well-known, or established a cartoonist may be, rejection slips remain a way of life for him.

"WHAT THE HELL ARE THESE BLASTED KIDS DOING IN SENIOR CITY?"

"BAH! WE'RE ALL NEUROTIC!"

"THAT'S HIS LATEST. HE CALLS IT 'BEYOND ART'"

PRIMITIVE ART AS INSPIRA-TION FOR CARTOONING

For me, primitive art and cartooning have a direct relationship, perhaps because I see both as products of the invisible world of the imagination. As I see it, the direct approach of primitive people to their art is similar to the way the cartoonists and caricaturists approach their world. Primitive art exhibits, whether in museums or private galleries, are favorite haunts of mine. They remain a major inspirational influence on my work.

Dell Publishing, 1964

CAMEROON-AFRICA

BAULE-AFRICA COLL. AL ROSS

Art is the result of a mixture of reality and imagination. In African art, imagination is foremost.

DOGON-AFRICA

BALEGA-CONGO, AFRICA. Collection Lee Lorenz.

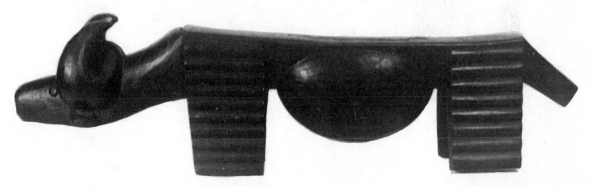

BAROTSE-RHODESIA, AFRICA.   Peabody Museum

CONGO-AFRICA   Royal African Museum

Actually African art is not a primitive art. It is a complete and perfect expression of a well defined mentality. It has been labled primitive because the people live a primitive existence. It is an art that, like Egyptian, Greek, Chinese, and Gothic art, has taken thousands of years of civilization to evolve and set.

DOGON-AFRICA

CONGO-AFRICA   Royal African Museum

Dell Publishing, 1964

Form is expressed by primitive people in its simplest properties; they approach it in its simplest terms, in geometrical figures of the different parts of which it is composed. In African sculpture each part of the whole keeps its individual significance in its function or action.

CAMEROON

CONGO-AFRICA   Royal African Museum

Here humor is combined with great finesse of balance and execution.

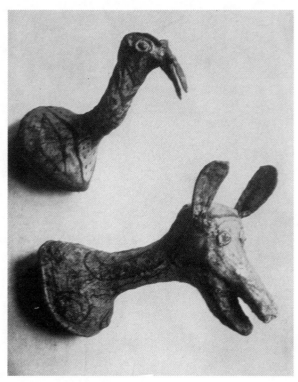

BRAZIL, 19TH CENTURY

Primitive people of Brazil created the above cartoony animals.

"Hey! Slow down!"

NEW YORKER, 1967

DOGON-AFRICA

DAN-AFRICA

DAN-AFRICA

DAN-AFRICA

Above are three examples of abstract African masks of the 19th Century. Below is a more realistic mask of the 20th Century.

MAKONDE-AFRICA

SATURDAY REVIEW, 1963

CAMEROON—AFRICA

To the left is a wonderfully expressionistic head, and below a similarly relaxed figure from New Zealand.

ASHANTI-AFRICA

NEW ZEALAND   Glasgow Museum

THE CARTOON AS FINE ART

Jean Dubuffet, the French painter, uses the child's world of fantasy as inspiration for his art. He combines it with a grotesque sense of humor.

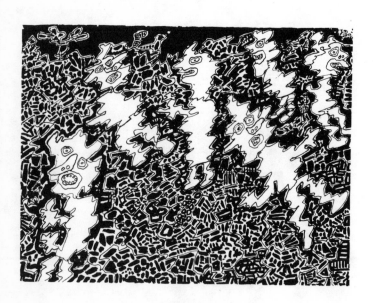

SENGAI—JAPAN

Japanese artists of the 12th and 13th Centuries did not think of themselves as cartoonists. But a glance at this page showing some of their remarkable cartoon-like work demonstrates again the indivisibility of cartooning and fine art.

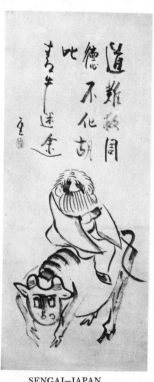

HAKUIN—JAPAN   SENGAI—JAPAN   SENGAI—JAPAN

Pablo Picasso made no distinction between the cartoon and fine art. On this and the facing page is a four-panel strip by the great master. Are they cartoons? Of course! Are they fine art? Naturally!

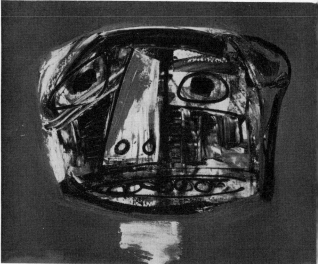

ANTONIO SAURA — SPAIN 1930   Collection Hy Klabenow

Antonio Saura, Spanish painter, uses violent
strokes to bring forth his grotesque cartoon-
like images.

DELL PUB., 1964

PAUL KLEE, 1940

In this painting, Paul Klee, as he had in all of his paintings, was aiming at a graphic art which could be defined as "the expressive movement of a hand equipped with a pencil to move it."

JOAN MIRÓ

Joan Miró expresses his world through graffiti-cartoon-like paintings.

MATERIALS

Drawing table: You can buy one that can be adjusted to suit you, or you can use a regular table that you have at home. Either can be utilized standing or sitting.

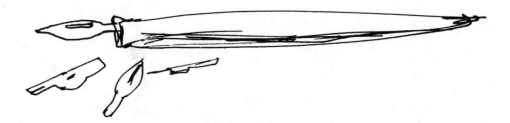

Pens: Try a variety until you find the one with which you get the best results.

You will also need india ink (black), brushes of various sizes, and white poster paint for touching up, with a white brush.

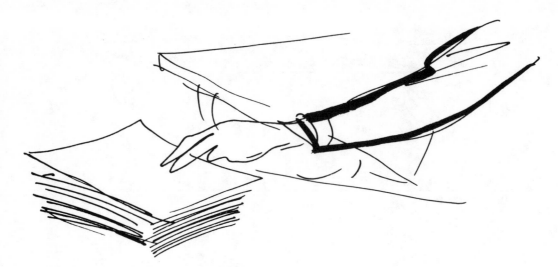

Rough paper

Keep a variety of pads of drawing paper on hand for doing your finished drawings. Also, have a tracing paper pad, very necessary for experimenting. Try illustration board—which is also good for wash, if you need a hard surface for your pen. By using a combination of materials you will find the one that is best suited for you.

Always keep a great number of pencils of different varieties around.
Also, crayons, pastels, erasers for pencil and ink, a kneaded eraser; a
pad for wash, plus a pad for color, or color tubes if you prefer; water
color brushes; and plenty of cups for mixing. A good thorough scan-
ning of materials at the art supply store will inspire you to buy a
variety of material to experiment with.

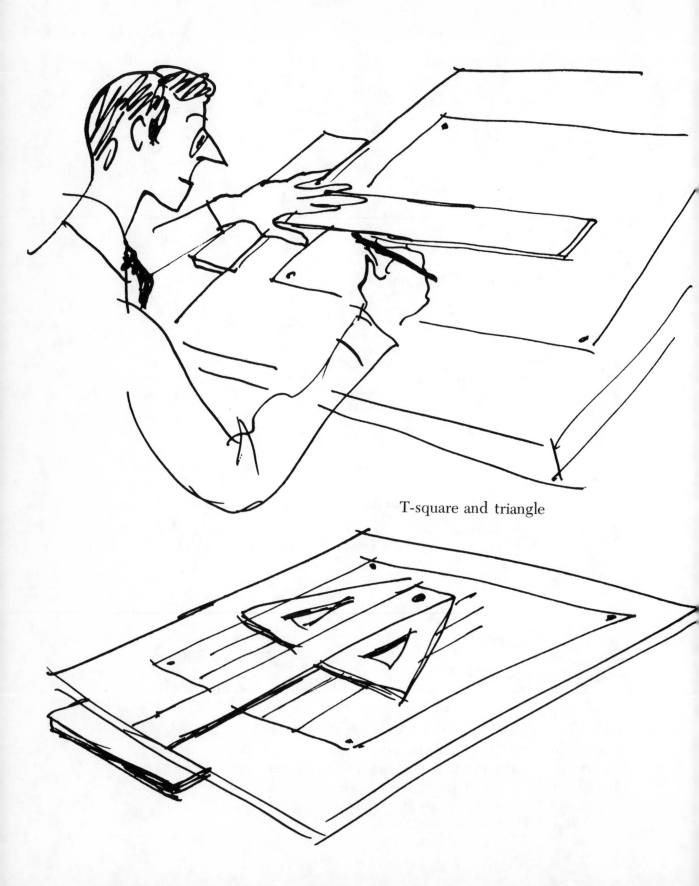

T-square and triangle

A moveable lamp is indispensable in an art studio.

You may not have cause to use a tracing box frequently, but there are times when it is a helpful time-saver.

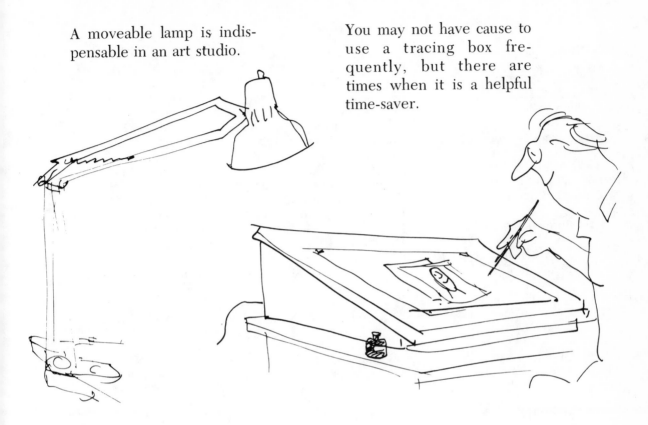

If you have the space, a table that can serve both as a work and storage area will keep the studio uncluttered. The flat table serves my personal style as frequently I prefer working standing up. It appears to me that drawing standing up gives my line a lot of freedom and spontaneity.

Of course, you will need a variety of inks.